12 WOMEN IN
SPORTS

by Marne Ventura

STORY LIBRARY
MORE TO EXPLORE

www.12StoryLibrary.com

12-Story Library is an imprint of Bookstaves.

Photographs ©: Tourism Victoria/CC2.0, cover, 1; Kathy Hutchins/Shutterstock.com, 4; Abdo Allam/Shutterstock.com, 5; Alex Livesey/CC2.0, 5; WENN Rights Ltd/Alamy, 6; PCN Photography/Alamy, 7; GEPA pictures/Mathias Mandl/PD, 8; dominika zarzycka/Shutterstock.com, 9; PD, 9; Kathy Hutchins/Shutterstock.com, 10; Lennox McLendon/Associated Press, 11; Naemajano/CC4.0, 12; Lorie Shaull/CC4.0, 13; Jay Godwin/PD, 14; Leonard Zhukovsky/Shutterstock.com, 15; Tourism Victoria/CC2.0, 16; Ike Li/Shutterstock.com, 17; PD, 18; PD, 19; Nicolas Economou/Shutterstock.com, 19; Debby Wong/Shutterstock.com, 20; action sports/Shutterstock.com, 21; WENN Rights Ltd/Alamy, 21; CBS This Morning/YouTube.com, 22; CBS This Morning/YouTube.com, 23; NBPA/CC4.0, 23; BLP Photos/PD, 24; Vitaliy Belousov/Associated Press, 25; JStone/Shutterstock.com, 26; Leonard Zhukovsky/Shutterstock.com, 27; Bain News Service/Library of Congress, 28; PD, 29

ISBN
9781632357847 (hardcover)
9781632358936 (paperback)
9781645820642 (ebook)

Library of Congress Control Number: 2019938614

Printed in the United States of America
September 2019

About the Cover
Li Na in 2015.

Access free, up-to-date content on this topic plus a full digital version of this book. Scan the QR code on page 31 or use your school's login at 12StoryLibrary.com.

Table of Contents

Simone Biles: Most Decorated Gymnast

Simone Biles has been called the best athlete in America. Born in 1997 in Columbus, Ohio, she had a tough early childhood. Her father was not around. Her mother had problems with alcohol and drugs. When Biles was three, she was put into foster care. Her grandfather and his wife adopted her. They have been her parents ever since.

Biles grew up near Houston, Texas. When she was six, she went on a school field trip to a gymnastics center. A coach noticed her copying the gymnasts' movements. He saw raw talent. The coach asked Biles's parents to enroll her in the center. Biles trained there for 11 years.

In 2010, Biles won a gold medal in floor exercise and a bronze medal in vault at the Women's Junior Olympics. That was the start of an amazing career. She was the first African American woman to win the all-around title at her first World Gymnastics Championships. She was the first woman ever to win five US Gymnastics all-around titles. (That was after a two-year break from competing.) She won five medals at the 2016 Olympic Games in Rio. Four of them were gold.

Simone Biles in 2016.

Biles has faced racism and risen above it to become the most decorated US gymnast in history. In 2018, she had the courage to come forward and say she had been abused.

25+

Number of world championship and Olympic medals Simone Biles has won

- Biles owns the most world medals in US history.
- She won her four all-around world titles in 2013, 2014, 2015, and 2018.
- In 2017, she made *Time* magazine's list of the world's 100 most influential people.

THINK ABOUT IT

Simone Biles showed talent for gymnastics at a very young age. She trains about 35 hours per week. Which do you think helped her succeed more—her talent or her hard work?

Bonnie Blair: Success under Pressure

Bonnie Blair in 2008.

knew they could count on her. A group of over 60 family members and friends cheered her on during her many victories. They were called the "Blair Bunch."

At the 1988 Calgary Olympics, Blair skated 500 meters faster than any woman ever had. With a record time of 39.1 seconds, she won the gold medal. Blair set a new goal of breaking the 39-second mark. She achieved it five years later, in March 1994, with a time of 38.99.

Bonnie Blair was an Olympic speed skater. Born in 1964 in Cornwall, New York, she came from a family of skaters. Like her five older brothers and sisters, she learned to skate when she was two. During her skating career, she was known for doing well under pressure. She always strove to do better, and she succeeded. Her teammates

At the 1992 Albertville Olympics, Americans were counting on Blair to win the 500-meter race. She beat her closest competitor, Ye Qiaobo of China, by 18 hundredths of a second. This win made Blair the first American woman ever to win consecutive gold medals at this event. Blair competed in speed skating until March of 1995. She now gives motivational speeches.

5

Number of Olympic gold medals Blair won by the time she retired

- Blair is known for her modesty and confidence.
- She also water skis, snow skis, plays golf and softball.
- Her most requested speech topic is "Achieving Your Personal Best."

MADE FOR SPEED

Blair was smaller than most speed skaters. She made up for her size with excellent technique. Her skating was very consistent. She was able to stay in a crouched low position. She pushed herself forward with long strides. She kept her strides in a smooth rhythm for the whole race.

Blair competing at the 1992 Albertville Olympics.

Mary Davis: Giving Everyone the Chance to Play

Mary Davis (right) congratulates Micol Jarmolinski on her giant slalom win at the 2017 Special Olympics.

Mary Davis is the head of Special Olympics. She was born in Ireland in 1954. After college, she became a PE teacher at a special education school. Davis loves sports. She believes everyone should have the chance to play. She has focused her life's work on bringing the joy of sports to people with intellectual disabilities. She wants them to be active. She wants them to be part of society. She wants them to feel as welcome and included as any other athlete.

Special Olympics is a program for people ages eight years and older with intellectual disabilities. It provides training and games in over 20 sports. Davis helped lead the 1985 Special Olympics in Europe. She became head of Special Olympics Ireland in 1989. In 2003, she led the first World Summer Games held outside the US. This was the world's largest sports event for that year.

HOW IT ALL BEGAN

Special Olympics got its start in the United States a few years before Davis got involved. Eunice Kennedy Shriver was President John F. Kennedy's sister. In 1962, she started a sports camp in Maryland for children with mental disabilities. More camps followed in the US and Canada. The first Special Olympics Games were held in Chicago in 1968.

In 2016, Davis was named head of Special Olympics International. She is the first non-American to lead the group. As a champion of athletes with intellectual disabilities, she has helped make Special Olympics a powerful organization that touches the lives of people around the world.

100,000
Number of competitions held each year by Special Olympics

- Special Olympics serves 6 million athletes.
- Over 1 million coaches and volunteers help with the Games.
- In 2003, Davis was named Irish Person of the Year for her service to Special Olympics.

Jackie Joyner-Kersee: Greatest Female Athlete

Some say Jackie Joyner-Kersee is the greatest female athlete ever. She was born Jacqueline Joyner in 1962 in East St. Louis, Illinois. She loved sports. In high school, she played on the volleyball, basketball, and track teams. She graduated near the top of her class. She set her high school's long jump record. She earned a scholarship to the University of California, Los Angeles (UCLA).

In 1981, she began training for the Olympics. She won the silver medal in the heptathlon in the 1984 Summer Games in Los Angeles. Her coach was Bob Kersee. They married in 1986. The same year, she set the world record for her event at the Goodwill Games in Russia. She set the world record for the fourth time at the 1988 Olympics in Seoul. She also won the gold medal. In 1992, in Barcelona, Spain, she became the first athlete to win her event at two Games in a row. Her last Olympic Games were in Atlanta in 1996. She earned a bronze medal.

Jackie Joyner-Kersee in 2018.

In 1988, Joyner-Kersee started a foundation for kids at risk in the town where she grew up. In 2007, she helped start Athletes for Hope. This group connects professional athletes with charities. In 2016, she helped create a program that provides internet access to low-income families.

Joyner-Kersee in the lead at the 1988 Summer Olympics.

HEPTATHLON

Joyner-Kersee's main event in the Olympics was the heptathlon. It is a track and field contest for female athletes. It includes seven events. Contestants do a 100-meter hurdle, a high jump, a shot put, a 200-meter dash, a long jump, a javelin throw, and an 800-meter run.

7,291
Points Jackie Joyner-Kersee earned in the 1988 heptathlon, a world record that still stands

- Joyner-Kersee earned three Olympic gold medals.
- She won four World Outdoor Championship gold medals.
- Her autobiography, *A Kind of Grace*, was published in 1997.

Maya Moore: Basketball Legend

Maya Moore with her MVP trophy in 2014.

Maya Moore is a professional basketball player. She was born in Missouri in 1989 to Kathryn Moore and Mike Dabney. Dabney is also a pro basketball player. Moore was raised by her mother. When she was three, she was always running around the apartment. Her mother put a basketball hoop on the back door to keep her busy. Moore has been shooting hoops ever since. Moore moved to Georgia with her mother when she was 11. She went to four different middle schools. She moved a hoop with her each time. She practiced every chance she got.

Moore went to the University of Connecticut from 2007 to 2011. She played forward on the basketball team and became team captain. Her team won national championships in 2009 and 2010. They won 90 games in a row, the most in college basketball history. Moore was named NCAA Academic All-American of the Year. In 2011, she was the first pick in the Women's National Basketball Association (WNBA) draft. She joined the Minnesota Lynx.

2016

Year when Maya Moore became the first athlete to win three WNBA titles in five seasons

- She won the ROY, All-Star MVP, and League MVP.
- She and the Olympics team won their sixth straight gold medal the same year.
- Moore also works to end childhood hunger and educate people about the unfair justice system.

Moore's team won the WNBA Championship in 2011. Moore was named WNBA Rookie of the Year (ROY) and All-Star Starter. In spring 2012, she won two championships in Europe. That summer, she won a gold medal with the US team at the Olympics.

Moore joined the women's basketball team in China in 2013. Her team won three years in a row. She led the Lynx to championships again in 2013, 2015, and 2017.

Ibtihaj Muhammad: Fencing Champion in a Hijab

Ibtihaj Muhammad is the first American athlete to compete in the Olympics wearing a hijab, or head scarf. Muhammad was born in 1985 in New Jersey. Her parents were African Americans who became Muslim. The rules of the religion call for women to cover their heads and bodies. Muhammad liked sports, but the uniforms made it hard for her to play. They were not modest enough. When Muhammad was 13, her mother suggested she try fencing. The fencing uniform fully covers the athlete's body.

Muhammad decided to try fencing. She hoped it would help her get into college.

Muhammad started to train at a local club. She didn't love fencing at first. But she stuck with it. In 1991, she learned about a fencing trainer in Harlem. She felt comfortable there. Most of the other athletes were African American. After high school, she got a scholarship to Duke University in North Carolina. She earned degrees in International Relations and African Studies. While at Duke, Muhammad rose to the top of the national rankings in fencing. She was named National Collegiate Athletic Association (NCAA) All-American three years in a row.

In 2011 and 2015, Muhammad's team won a gold medal in the Pan American Games. She won five medals in the World Championships between 2013 and 2015. At the 2016 Olympics in Rio, Muhammad won the bronze medal.

Ibtihaj Muhammad in 2018.

2014

Year when Ibtihaj Muhammad launched her own modest fashion brand

- In 2018, the Mattel toy company made a Barbie doll modeled after Muhammad.
- Muhammad is a sports ambassador for the US government.
- She is an advocate for equal rights in sports.

Muhammad claims victory at the 2016 Olympics in Rio.

THINK ABOUT IT

Ibtihaj Muhammad is best known for wearing a hijab during the Olympic Games. Why do you think this got more attention than her skill at fencing?

Li Na: Trailblazing Tennis Player

Li Na is a Chinese tennis player. She was born in 1982 in Wuhan, a city in Central China. The Chinese government runs the sport system. Li's father signed her up for badminton. The coach suggested tennis. At the time, few people in China knew about tennis. Li's parents called it "fuzzy ball." By the time she was eight, Li practiced six days a week. Her coach was harsh and critical. She grabbed Li's arm and scolded her often. This was the way of most Chinese coaches.

Li's father died while she was playing in a tournament at age 14. Her mother didn't tell her until after the tournament. Li was angry and devastated. At 15, she became the youngest person ever to win the National League Singles Finals. But she was not happy. Her mother had remarried. She had gone into debt. Li met Jaing Shaan, another tennis player. He became Li's boyfriend and later her husband.

In 2008, Li beat champion US player Venus Williams in the Beijing Olympics. After that, she fought for and won more freedom from the government system. She was able to choose her own coach. She got to keep more of her prize money.

Li Na in 2015.

2014

Year when Li Na was the world's highest-paid athlete

- In 2011, Li was the first tennis player from Asia to win a Grand Slam singles title at the French Open.
- In 2019, she was the first Asian player inducted into the International Tennis Hall of Fame in Rhode Island.
- She made tennis a popular sport in China.

In 2014, Li won her second Grand Slam championship. She was Number 2 in the Women's Tennis Association rankings, right behind Serena Williams. Soon after, Li retired from tennis. She had knee injuries. She wanted to start a family. Li and her husband now have a daughter and a son.

Samia Yusuf Omar: Determined to Run

Omar made it to the 2008 Olympics. The other athletes wore slick new workout clothes. Omar wore long black leggings, a too-big T-shirt, and shoes donated by the team from Sudan. The crowd cheered for her spirit and effort. Upon her return, the military group that ruled Somalia threatened Omar. They said Muslim women should not be athletes.

Samia Yusuf Omar in 2008.

Samia Yusuf Omar was a sprinter. She was born in Somalia, Africa, in 1991. Her country has had many years of war, drought, and famine. Omar quit school in eighth grade, after her father died. She helped with her younger siblings. Omar dreamed of running in the Olympics. She trained in a bombed-out stadium. The track was full of potholes. Often soldiers scared her into going home.

21
Samia Yusuf Omar's age when she died

- Had she survived, Omar might have been part of the first-ever refugee team at the Rio Olympics in 2016.
- She hoped becoming an Olympic athlete would give her family a better life.
- Her loss has inspired her Somali teammates to fight for reform.

The book, *An Olympic Dream*, about the challenges Omar faced, was published in 2016.

REFUGEE CRISIS

People like Samia Yusuf Omar who flee their homes are called refugees. Most are from the Middle East, South Asia, East Africa, and West Africa. Refugees are escaping war, danger, hunger, and disease. They are looking for a new home where they can build a better life.

Women were supposed to cover their bodies with robes in public.

Omar left Somalia in 2010. She traveled to Libya to train for the 2012 Olympics. In April 2012, Omar and 70 other people boarded a small, flimsy boat. They were trying to get to Italy. Somewhere along the way, Omar fell overboard and drowned. Her tragic death raised awareness of the hardships faced by female athletes in Somalia. Omar is a symbol of resilience and determination.

Danica Patrick: Champion Race Car Driver

Danica Patrick is the most successful woman race car driver ever. Born in Wisconsin in 1982, she grew up in Illinois. She tried many sports and activities as a child. When she was 10, her family took up go-kart racing. On her first drive, Patrick crashed into a wall. Her jacket caught on fire. But she loved racing. She raced often in local and national events. She won titles. When she was 16, she got the chance to go to England to train and race. She stayed for three years.

229.88

Danica Patrick's lap time in miles per hour (370 km/hr) during an Indy practice in 2005, the fastest ever

- Patrick was named Rookie of the Year for 2005.
- She was voted Indy Racing League Most Popular Driver in 2005, 2006, and 2007.
- Since retiring, she has written several books and started two businesses.

Danica Patrick in 2012.

Patrick's car (10) in the lead at the NASCAR Cup Series pole in 2013.

POLE AWARD
FEBRUARY 17, 2013

When Patrick got back to the United States, she joined a professional racing team. In May 2005, she led 19 laps and came in fourth in her first Indianapolis 500. She was the first woman to lead laps and score a top-five finish. In 2008, she was the first woman to win a major-league open-wheel race in a North American series in Japan.

In 2013, Patrick entered the NASCAR Cup Series. She became the first female to win a NASCAR Cup Series pole. She set the record for fastest time in qualifying for the Daytona 500. When she finished in eighth place, it was the highest rank in history for a woman. Patrick had the most top-10 finishes of any woman in the NASCAR Cup in 2015. In 2017, she raced in the Daytona 500 and the Indianapolis 500. She called it the "Danica Double." After that, she retired.

Michele Roberts: Fighting for the Players

Michele Roberts is an African American lawyer. She was born in 1956 in the Bronx to a single mother. Roberts got her law degree at the University of California. She worked as a trial attorney in Washington, DC, for over 30 years. She was known for her loyalty to her clients. Juries liked her. Some people said she was the best trial lawyer in DC.

In July 2014, the National Basketball Players Association (NBPA) chose Roberts to be its head. The NBPA is a union. Its purpose is to protect the rights of professional basketball players. When Roberts took over, she became the first female leader of a sports labor union.

The former director had just been fired. The players were trying to get more pay and better schedules. The last time players and team owners had a big disagreement, the owners locked out the players. All the games were cancelled. The players could not play. The lockout lasted for 149 days.

Michele Roberts in 2016.

CBS THIS MORNING

HOLDING COURT
NBA UNION CHIEF BREAKS BASKETBALL'S GLASS CEILING

THINK ABOUT IT

When Michele Roberts became the first female head of a major US sports union, people gave her credit for "shattering a glass ceiling." What does this mean? Why is it important?

That didn't happen this time. By 2016, Roberts reached a deal with the National Basketball Association (NBA). She got the players what they wanted. That agreement will stay in place through 2024.

2018
Year when Michele Roberts was chosen for another four-year term as NBPA Executive Director

- Roberts earns a base salary of $1.2 million per year.
- She gets letters from people thanking her for being a role model.
- She fell in love with basketball as a child watching the New York Knicks.

Fatma Samba Diouf Samoura: World Soccer Leader

Fatma Samba Diouf Samoura is a leader in the World Soccer Association (FIFA). Soccer is the world's most popular sport. This makes Samoura one of the most powerful women in sports today.

Samoura was born in 1962 in Senegal. In her Muslim culture, many parents only sent their sons to school. Samoura's parents made sure she got a good education. After high school, she studied in France. By age 25, she earned three graduate degrees. Back in Senegal, she worked for the United Nations (UN) for 21 years. She helped start and lead humanitarian programs around the world.

In 2016, Samoura became secretary-general of FIFA. Her position is second to the president. She is the first woman to hold this job. When she came to FIFA, she had no experience working in sports. She was hired for her leadership skills.

Fatma Samba Diouf Samoura in 2018.

Samoura spreads her message that soccer is a way to unite those who have differences.

Samoura sees soccer as a way to unite people. During her work for the UN, she saw how sports helped troubled communities. People came together as a team. They took a break from their problems during a soccer game. Playing together was a way to unite those with differences.

Number 1

Fatma Samoura's rank on *Forbes'* Most Powerful Women in International Sports list

- Samoura speaks four languages.
- She wants soccer to be inclusive for all people.
- Samoura says her group is like the UN of soccer because it brings people together.

FOOTBALL OR SOCCER?

In North America, Australia, and part of Africa, the sport is called soccer. Samoura and the rest of the world call it football. In the 19th century, players in the United Kingdom named it "association football." American players shortened that to "soccer," a slang term that started with the "soc" in association.

Serena Williams: Tennis Icon

Serena Williams in 2018.

23

Record-setting number of Grand Slam singles titles Serena Williams has won during the Open Era

- Williams has redefined tennis fashion with her stylish, unique outfits.
- She launched her own line of clothing in 2018.
- She encourages strong, muscular women to be proud of their looks.

Serena Williams is an African American tennis player. She was born in 1981 in Saginaw, Michigan, and grew up in Compton, a poor section of Los Angeles. Her father coached her and her sister Venus on public courts. Serena played in her first match when she was four years old. By the time she was 12, she was ranked Number 1 in her age group.

Two young, talented, female African American tennis players, Serena and Venus got lots of attention from the media. In 1999, Serena became the first African American woman to win the Grand Slam singles title at the US Open. She was 18 years old.

The Williams sisters won gold medals in the doubles event at the 2000 Olympics in Australia. Between 2002 and 2014, Serena won five more titles at the US Open. In 2015, she won her sixth Australian Open and the French Open. In 2016, she won at Wimbledon. In 2017, at the Australian open, Serena set a new record for Grand Slam single titles.

Serena has changed the world of tennis, a sport historically played by wealthy whites. Along with her sister Venus, she has inspired African American kids to play tennis. She is known for her grace, good sportsmanship, and humility.

TENNIS TERMS

Tennis has four big contests. They are called Grand Slams. One is in Australia and the others are in France, England, and the United States. When a player wins all four, it's called a Career Grand Slam. An Open tennis match is one where amateurs as well as professionals can compete.

Williams in action at the 2018 Grand Slam.

Out of the Shadows

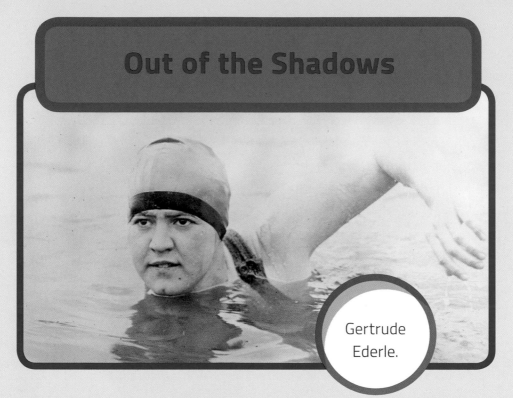

Gertrude Ederle.

Gertrude Ederle

Gertrude Ederle was born in New Jersey in 1905. She set many records as an amateur swimmer and won a gold medal at the 1924 Olympic Games in Paris. In 1925, she became the first woman to swim the English Channel. She beat the men's world record time by 1 hour 59 minutes.

Wilma Rudolph

Born in Tennessee in 1940, Wilma Rudolph overcame crippling childhood polio to become an athlete. In 1960, she earned the title "Fastest Woman in the World" when she became the first American woman to win three gold medals in track and field at the same Olympic Games in Rome.

Madge Syers with her husband Edgar.

Madge Syers

Madge Syers was an English figure skater and the first woman to enter the world championship. The year was 1902. The judges banned female competitors because long skirts blocked their feet from view. Syers started a trend by wearing a shorter skirt. In 1908, she won the Olympic gold medal.

Norma Wilson

Norma Wilson was a sprinter from New Zealand. In 1928, she was the first woman sprinter to compete in the 100-meter race at the Olympics. That was in Amsterdam. Wilson made it to the semifinals. In London the same year, she won an international race.

Glossary

amateur
A person who competes in a sport without getting paid.

Bronx
A section of New York City known for gangs and poverty in the 1900s.

client
A person who hires a professional such as a lawyer.

foster care
A home given to children whose parents can't take care of them.

Harlem
A large neighborhood in New York City known as the center of African American art and culture.

humanitarian
Done to help people who are in need or suffering.

kids at risk
Children who don't have a good support system to help them succeed in school and in life.

lockout
When employers don't let workers come to work unless the workers agree to certain conditions.

modest
Clothing that doesn't show too much of a woman's body.

Muslim
An Arabic religion.

polio
A disease caused by a virus that can cause paralysis.

union
An organization of workers who unite to protect their rights and interests.

United Nations
An international organization formed in 1945 to promote worldwide peace and security.

Read More

Amson-Bradshaw, Georgia. *Incredible Sporting Champions*. New York: Barron's, 2018.

Ignotofsky, Rachel. *Women in Sports: 50 Fearless Athletes Who Played to Win.* Berkeley, CA: Ten Speed Press, 2017.

Zuckerman, Gregory, and Gabriel Zuckerman. *Rising Above: Inspiring Women in Sports*. New York: Philomel Books, 2018.

Visit 12StoryLibrary.com

Scan the code or use your school's login at **12StoryLibrary.com** for recent updates about this topic and a full digital version of this book. Enjoy free access to:

- Digital ebook
- Breaking news updates
- Live content feeds
- Videos, interactive maps, and graphics
- Additional web resources

Note to educators: Visit 12StoryLibrary.com/register to sign up for free premium website access. Enjoy live content plus a full digital version of every 12-Story Library book you own for every student at your school.

Index

About the Author

Marne Ventura has written over 100 books for children. A former elementary school teacher, she holds a master's degree in education from the University of California. Marne and her husband live on the central coast of California.